THE LAST RAIN FOREST

Legend of the Green Man

Written by
Felipe Moreton Chohfi

Illustrations by Angelo Bonito

19th July, 2014.

Pat.

Enjoy the Green Man !

Vermilion Pencil Press

Concord, New Hamphsire

The Last Rain Forest
Legend of the Green Man
By
Felipe Chohfi

Illustrated by Angelo Bonito

Book design by Pam Marin-Kingsley, Grey Gate Media, LLC

Extra illustrations in How You Can Help Save the Rain Forest section from:
Rio santiago poison-dart frog : artist: artyuten, www.vectorstock.com
Toucan: artist: Josef Prchal, www.123rf.com
All other animals: artist: insima, www.123rf.com

1st Paperback Edition
Printed in the U.S.A.

Paperback ISBN 13: 978-1-61807-089-0
ePub ISBN: 978-1-61807-090-6
Library of Congress Control Number: 2012949871

Vermillion Pencil Press
an imprint of Grey Gate Media, LLC
Concord, New Hampshire
email: info@greygatemedia.com
www.greygatemedia.com

I would like to dedicate this book to my grandfather, Allen Frederick Moreton Treacher, for having believed in me.

Dear grandfather, you are the one who gave me hope and made me understand that this book had the potential to be published. Thank you very much for your knowledgeable arguments, I will never forget.

To God, our Creator for his goodness in giving me this blessing that has come from above.

Acknowledgements

First to my mother for presenting me the opportunity of rediscovering this book I had written as a child, and standing by me throughout the writing process. Rewriting this book was very important for me, not only as a memory, but to better know myself. Thank you so much mummy for your assistance.

Thank you Donald Michael Platt for sharing your experience as a writer and helping me to create a readable work of fiction.

Special thanks to my father for always being so understanding and reassuring in my life, and for having taught me most everything I know.

Many, many thanks to Angelo Bonito for reading the book and creating the illustrations that brought the story to life.

I have no words to explain my gratitude to all of you, family, friends, my wife Evana and my sister for showing your approval.

Thanks to Pam and the Grey Gate Media, LLC for having made the publishing possible.

Chapter 1
Getting to Know Me

My name is Mathias Gianni and I am twelve years old. I live in the south of Brazil, one of the largest countries in the world. I enjoy swimming, playing tennis, golf, soccer, and computer games with my friends at the British school where I study. I do not go out at night though. I prefer to stay in the mansion where I live and watch television, mostly nature programs, after I finish my homework.

Often I daydream and take walks alone without having anywhere I really have to go. My mother says I live in a world of my own.

Although my father expects me to join him in his business after I complete my schooling, I hope one day to become an ecologist. I am passionately concerned about protecting our natural environment and its endangered animal and plant species.

My father, Frank Gianni, owns large factories in many countries. He may be the richest and most powerful man in the world. He influences and even controls many governments.

The Gianni multinational industries are continually expanding because of the large demand for their products. Gianni owns airlines, shipping, cellulose, energy and agro-industries. Gianni also manufactures all types of things: paper, toys, cars, bottles, watches, shoes, rubber and even food.

In every home, most items have a capital "G" for Gianni; my favorite is a chocolate bar called *Gianniolate*.

I am an only child, and sometimes my mother is over-protective of me. She constantly watches what I do and who I am with. My dad is away most of the time because he travels all over the world to supervise his businesses. Although I love him and miss him a lot, right now I am angry with him. Gianni Industries are destroying natural forests all over the world for the raw materials needed to manufacture its products and to create open space for farming, beef breeding, more factories and their supporting cities.

Rain forests used to cover our planet in the equatorial regions, and, I am sorry to say, my father is now responsible for depleting the last of them. Few people care about those forests because they want his products. No government will stop him. No organized environmental group can stop him. I wish I could, but even though I am his son, he will not listen to me.

A few years ago, my former Nanny, who had spent many years working as a nurse deep inside the Amazon rain forest, came to visit us. Because she knew how I felt about the environment, she told me about the legend of the Green Man. She said when the last rain forests were about to be destroyed, he would rise with the power to turn humans into trees if they did not heed his warning to stop the cutting.

Chapter 2
My Father's Plans

After my father returned from his latest trip in South America, he showed me a map of northwestern Brazil. "Mathias, here is where I acquired the last untouched rain forest."

"Father, that is fantastic,!" I said, thinking like an environmentalist. 'Then surely you must be thinking of making it a nature preserve to conserve it for future generations."

"No, son, I shall cut it down so I can convert its resources into Gianni goods and increase our wealth. Trust me, Mathias. One day you will do the same."

"How can I do such a thing if this is the *LAST* rain forest? And why would I do such a thing? How much money do we need? I would rather share the forest with others, and give it as a gift."

I was shocked and disappointed. I began to imagine a world with no forests. Couldn't he see that all the forests would be gone by the time I became an adult?

Where were his heart and his love for the world around him?

"Dad, did you know a Green Man exists? He will rise when there are nearly no more forests left. He has the power to turn people into trees," I tried to warn him.

My father laughed, "Money most of all, and the power it brings rules the earth—not some mythical green monster. Son, your Green Man is just a silly legend. Our family industries have been cutting forests for over a

century, and no Green Man has ever appeared. I shall begin the logging in the rain forest in two months."

My father's plans for the last rain forest distressed me. Large stretches of forest are necessary because they supply oxygen for us to breathe. They also help regulate temperatures in our atmosphere. I had already learned our planet's climate had changed for the worst during the past decades. The North and South Poles had melted, and half the white land mass that was formerly Antarctica was beginning to turn green.

Domes now covered all the great cities of the world. People needed to carry oxygen dispensers with them so they could breathe. Not surprising, my father's company made these machines. Although he had many tree planting programs underway, I knew they were inadequate and these trees were merely there to make things look pretty.

I believed my Father's ambitions could destroy all human life on earth. I had to think of something to stop him before it was too late.

Chapter 3
The Decision

I wrote to every Government, TV station, and newspaper warning them the destruction of the last rain forest could lead to the extinction of all human life on our planet. I received no replies. I even did a blog on the Internet and pod-casted my ideas for everyone to hear—but nothing happened. No one contacted me.

Even though everyone knew I was Frank Gianni's son, no one took me seriously. Like my father, they assumed I was just a kid with big dreams and ideas, and that the only thing I wanted was attention.

I became frustrated and desperate. I didn't know what to do next. Then I had an inspiration: What if my dad was wrong and the Green Man was not a myth? He or It would be the only possible force capable of preventing the destruction of the rain forests.

Despite my research in libraries and on the Internet, I had never found any evidence of a real Green Man who could turn whole populations into forests. Yet there was mention of him in the folk tales and legends of ancient Europe and other places like India, the Middle East, and Indonesia. So, I was confident he did exist. I had to believe because the Green Man was my only hope.

I used the savings from my allowance and sneaked out of my house without telling my mother. I booked a flight to northwestern Brazil to be there for the day of the first cutting. I looked forward to seeing an equatorial forest for the first time and discovering if the Green Man really existed.

My destination was the largest city in the world, Gianniopolis. While flying over Brazil, I observed from the airplane's window where the large, green stretches of forests my Nanny had described to me no longer existed. I saw in their places over-populated cities and towns, networks of roads, and beef, chicken and pork breeding farms and immense crop plantations with only tiny clusters of decorative trees.

As my plane approached Gianniopolis Airport, I was thrilled to see what had to be the last rain forest bordering a wide river. The trees were huge and green, and their canopy from above looked like a giant umbrella, protecting the earth. I had never seen anything so beautiful.

At the same time, I was horrified by all the construction and destruction going on at the forest's borders. Gianniopolis was expanding like a giant amoeba and was about to consume the last rain forest.

When we prepared to land, a flight attendant announced over the speaker, "All Gianni employees please exit through the front door of the plane. A bus is waiting to take you to your final destination."

I expected many Gianni employees to be on this flight. My father owned the airline, and many people were traveling to Gianniopolis to see the first day of cutting.

Was I the only one who cared about what was going to be destroyed?

Chapter 4
The Adventure Begins

When I got off the plane, I saw hundreds of environmentalists protesting against Gianni Industries. They were holding signs and shouting: "Save the forest. We need oxygen. We hate Gianni industries."

Many of the protestors were barefoot, and some almost naked. I remembered my Nanny's stories and photos in books about the Amazon and identified them as the natives who lived in the rain forest.

I went to the leaders of the protest and identified myself. I tried to convince them that I was the only person able to change my father's mind. They doubted even I could do that. They pointed to the armed guards and electrified fences surrounding the forest.

I also saw thousands of workers setting up machines for the day of the cutting. The sun glinted threateningly off the sharp metal blades of the machines—and I shivered despite the sun being high in the sky overhead.

I told them that the Green Man would appear and save the forest, but no one even among the environmentalists believed he existed. To prove me wrong, they snuck me into the forest's edge along the river.

My first sight of a rain forest thrilled me. I could distinguish a wide diversity of tree and plant species. The height of the trees and their leaves, fruits, and branches created a canopy so thick they blocked the sun. The dark was was cool and refreshing.

The trees must have taken centuries to grow. Some had roots spreading everywhere under the soil. They were nothing like the small clusters of decorative trees I was used to seeing. Thanks to my studies, I also could identify animal and insect species whose colors blended into the branches, leaves, flowers, and trunks of trees and plants.

The sound of the birds and rustling of the trees excited me. I had never breathed air so pure. The world must have looked like this after it had just been created, and before the first humans ever appeared.

"I believe in you, Green Man. Please stop the cutting! Save the trees, the animals and us," I called out to him. My environmentalist friends tried to calm me, but I pulled away and ran deeper into the forest, and fell as my feet got slippery and wet on the mud. While trying to stand up I saw what looked to be the curves of a tree trunk.

When I finally stopped, I saw a native girl with a monkey on top of her head. As she came nearer, I couldn't stop staring. Close to my age, she had short black hair and smooth brown skin, shining like polished noble wood.

Everything she wore came from the rain forest. The green strips of material barely covering her body were leaves of banana trees. She also wore a white necklace possibly made from real alligator teeth. The flowers covering her hair fascinated me.

I had never seen a girl like her in all my life. She looked as if she came from another world. Even the language she spoke as the other natives joined us, sounded strange. It had nothing to do with Brazilian Portuguese or the English and French I was learning in school.

My feelings towards the girl confused me. I wanted to meet her, get to know her. I was pleased when I saw her looking intently at me. Did she find me interesting, too?

Later, my new environmentalist friends told me her name was "Ayira." Her name meant, "Daughter of the Forest" in her own language. Her people were from the Amazon region. They said she had been born and raised in the rain forest and was now an orphan. Her parents had been run over and killed by cutting machines while defending another forest. Because Ayira had nowhere else to go, and could not return to the center of the forest, she had joined the protesters.

Chapter 5
A Final Plea

The following day I went to the corporate headquarters of Gianni industries and identified myself. Security guards immediately took me to my father's office, and he was delighted to see me. At that moment, I was happy because we were together. My dad promised we would take a family holiday after he cut down the last tree. But I wondered where we could go that would be as beautiful as the rain forest.

"You know, Father, there may be nowhere worth going after the last rain forest is gone. And if the Green Man is real, we will all have roots and not be able to move," I said solemnly.

"Nothing and no one can stop Gianni Industries from cutting down that forest. So we will go somewhere wonderful. You have nothing to worry about." Then my father laughed.

On the way to his penthouse in the city's tallest building, my father said he had a surprise for me. As soon as I walked into the apartment, my mother hugged and kissed me—she was the surprise.

"I did not know where you had gone. I thought you had been kidnapped," she told me. "I am so glad you are all right. You are too young to be traveling alone."

I tried to convince my mother the Green Man would stop my father if he tried to cut down the last rain forest.

"How can you believe such a thing?" she said. "You should not worry about the whole world or even your father. We have our own private army to protect us from any Green Thing. We are safer than anyone else can be."

But I disagreed.

No army could protect us. Unless I did something, every human being would die from lack of oxygen or be turned into a tree.

Chapter 6
The Night of the Appearance

That night while I slept, a deep voice called my name. "Mathias, come into the forest now, for I wish to speak with you."

I opened my eyes wider in the dark and saw green phosphorescent eyes. I knew it was the Green Man, and I was not afraid of him. Fully awake, I realized I was standing in the middle of the rain forest before an enormous creature who was part-tree and part-man.

"Mathias, you are a good boy and will grow into a fine man. You have a wonderful heart, and a pure soul. You believe in me, and you have done all you can to save this forest."

I was unable to speak in the presence of so awesome a being.

"I know you want to know everything about me. I am the first tree on earth, and my duty is to protect all forests. To do that, the Creator gave me limbs, a face, the gift of speech, and whatever powers I would need if and when humans would try to cut down the last rain forest. At this time, I am obliged to rise and transform all people into trees, to start the world all over again."

I had trouble understanding what I was hearing.

"The whole world will be a forest?" I said.

"Not exactly. I need boys like you to start the world all over again from the beginning, this time to ensure humans will live in harmony with the forests. If you decide to do so, you should have many children and educate them and their children's children regarding the role of the forests. What your father and others have done must not happen again."

Although I was still twelve-years-old, I understood I could not begin repopulating the world all by myself. The Green Man read my thoughts:

"You must choose a girl to live in the forested world with you, a girl who respects and loves the forest as much as you and who is not blinded by ambition and greed."

I thought carefully about the girls I had known in school who appealed to me. However, they would never adjust to living in a forest once they had known the modern world with all its conveniences and material goods. Besides, even though they were so beautiful, the attraction I felt for them did not compare to what I felt for a girl who never left my mind from the day I first saw her.

"Yes, Green Man, I have already chosen a girl. She comes from the rain forest. Her name is Ayira."

"That pleases me because I wanted you to choose her. Now pay attention, I need your help to use my powers. I cannot act unless you decide to summon me. To do that, you must use your imagination. I have the ability to take the shape of any tree in the rain forest. Just choose a tree and think of me. Then I shall appear and become what you wish. Your imagination has brought me to life. Know that I have power over all trees of the forest. However, I need your mind to tell me how to use my powers in every possible way when you summon me."

I agreed to do my part, but perhaps too quickly. I began to worry about my parents and school friends. "Please, Green Man, don't disappear. Tell me … do we really have to turn everyone into trees?"

"I must turn everyone who is not pure of heart, Mathias, in order to save the world. If they do not see what you and I see, they must become trees. And I will not hide the truth from you. After you summon me, the first to become trees in the forest shall be your parents and all Gianni employees, but we may yet spare them if they listen to me."

I did not want my parents to die. "Can you fix my father's brain and change his mind?"

"He has been given free will. I cannot change his mind or heart. He must do all that himself."

The Green Man said no more, and I awoke alone in my bedroom.

Chapter 7
The Day They Cut Down the Forest

The following morning, my parents took me with them to see the great cutting of the last rain forest. Media arrived from all over the world. So did thousands of protestors. A heavily armed security force protected my father and his workers, and helicopter gun-ships hovered above us. Their orders were shoot-to-kill. My father and mother wore camouflage fatigues and Teflon armor. I refused to wear the suit they had prepared for me.

I was concerned for my parents. I loved them. I did not want them to become trees. But I also wanted the Green Man to save the rain forest and all of humanity as well. I pleaded one last time with my father and mother, but they would not listen to me. Instead, my father faced the TV cameras and spoke for the entire world to hear:

"Today I shall begin the cutting down of the last rain forest," my father said. "This project is not just important for Gianni Industries, but for all of us." He phasized the economic benefits, which, I knew, would please all who heard him except the environmentalists.

At the conclusion of his speech, he held me closely in front of the cameras and said, "Green Man, or whatever you are; we are prepared for your tricks as well. So, if you really exist come out and show yourself."

Everyone laughed, but I became angry and worried. I knew it was not a good idea to annoy the Green Man.

A great silence came over everything. My father walked to the edge of the forest, toward a centenary tree. Everyone followed him, except the

environmentalists and natives from the forest. He looked at his watch and faced the cameras again.

"I want to have the pleasure to cut down the first tree in the old-fashioned way using a conventional ax. After that, my workers will move in with the heavy machines and begin eradicating the entire rain forest," he said.

I immediately ran away from him and searched for Ayira. I worried for her safety. Did the Green Man remember I had chosen her? I wanted to hold her hand when the cutting began. I had to protect her.

Security guards tookme back to my father before I found Ayira. Then I remembered my talk with the Green Man. To save the forest, I would have to summon him.

Calmer and more confident, I took my place beside my father ready to begin my work. He walked to a great Brazilian Nut Tree, over a century old and more than two hundred feet high. When he swung his ax into its thick trunk, I imagined the Green Man. The blade shattered, and we heard a tremendous clamor.

The Green Man appeared. Standing, he was taller than the Nut Tree and his voice boomed so loud, it was heard by all.

"Doctor Gianni, I have come to stop you from destroying this forest. If you refuse, I shall turn you and everyone else in the world into trees."

Upon seeing the Green Man, my father yelled, "It's a trick. Maybe it's a hologram created by these tree lovers. Shoot him! Destroy it!"

At that moment, I used my imagination to give the Green Man armor, and I added an invisible shield over the entire forest.

My father's army fired automatic rifles at the Green Man. His tanks and artillery shot shells. His planes dropped bombs and fired missiles. Nothing penetrated the Green Man's defenses, nor could anything or anyone harm the last rain forest.

Slowly, the Green Man grew taller. He fired laser beams from his green eyes. Helicopters crashed. Tanks and armored vehicles dissolved. Hand held weapons disappeared.

Everyone screamed and tried to run away from the Green Man, my parents too. Then I imagined all the trees of the forest entwining people with their roots and branches.

The Green Man caught my mother and father, and held them in each of his hands. He lifted my father up high, until they were face-to-face. "Frank

Gianni, you did not heed my warning. You decided to destroy the rain forest. Now you and all the other people like you shall become trees."

I could not have imagined what happened next. The Green Man vanished still holding my parents. Except for Ayira and me, all the people around us disappeared. So did the entire city of Gianniopolis.

Dense forests took its place. The same happened everywhere throughout the world—leaving very few of us left to restart the world again. Regardless of importance, age and gender, innocence and guilt regarding the destruction of the forests, almost every human being became a tree. Those of us left around the world had believed in one thing: The Green Man and his message.

Chapter 8
Living in a World that's a Forest

I cried because I had lost my parents. I loved them very much. I cried because no one could see the truth before the Green Man came. But, because he had transformed the world, I had no choice but to live in it with Ayira.

Then the Green Man appeared to us and began his important teachings.

"Never take more than what you need from the forest. You may eat any fruit, except from the tallest tree at the edge of the Amazon River. That tree contains the soul of Frank Gianni. If you eat its fruit, blind ambition and greed will enter your hearts and you and your descendants will begin to destroy the forests the same as your father and ancestors did."

After Ayira and I promised to do all the Green Man had asked, he disappeared never to be seen again. He went to teach the others—in other parts of the world. We would never meet them, but someday our children would.

For now, Ayira and I seemed the only two flesh and blood humans existing in a forested world, a world without endangered species. Animals were abundant, as well as fruits in the trees, fish in the river, swarms of vividly colored insects, and clusters of intensely fragrant flowers.

Did I imagine Ayira and I could speak the same language, or had the Green Man made it happen? I would never know. I walked and talked with her and observed our images in the clear waters of the river. I couldn't stop looking at her lovely face and graceful movements.

Ayira had much knowledge of the rain forest. She knew how to find food and shelter and understood the medicinal power of many plants. She could imitate the sounds animals made and determine the time of day simply by looking at the sun.

Ayira guided me into building our house to protect us from wild animals. Because I could lift more than she could, I did all the heavy work. When we had finished, it looked more like a hut made of wood and dry leaves—nothing like the luxurious high-tech home I had once lived in.

I had to learn to hunt and fish for food. How was I to do all that? At home, I had an unlimited choice of food cooked offered to me by our chef and servants. Now I had nothing left from my past life and no servants, except my own two hands. Even my favorite tennis shoes had disappeared. I had to walk and run on bare feet.

Ayira had much wisdom. She knew I would learn faster from experience. She said, "I don't want to be the one to catch wild frogs and gather fruits for meals every day. At least you should be able to fish for us."

I rushed to the river. Without a rod or even a knife, I decided to use the sharpest stick I could find. By the time I returned, the sun had set. I had returned empty handed. Many insect bites and cuts covered my face and body, and I had a strange numb feeling in my arm.

When I saw Ayira, it seemed she was furious with me. Her eyes opened wide, and she roughly seized my arm.

"Mathias. Hurry. Come here and drink this," she said handing me a wooden cup.

I drank the foul tasting liquid. The drink she gave me put me to sleep. When I awakened the next day, Ayira told me she had prepared an antidote from a plant of the rain forest for the snakebite that could have killed me.

"Sometimes they are so small, you cannot even feel their bite," she lectured me to be more careful.

"I was a city boy," I told her and described how pampered I was in my old life. In the rain forest, nothing would be easy for me any more.

Ayira then understood why I could not immediately adapt to life in a rain forest. "Don't worry," We will learn from each other. Otherwise, the Green Man would not have chosen you."

Ayira's reasoning gave me more confidence, but still, we urgently needed to discover what I could do.

A sudden equatorial rainstorm flooded and destroyed our fragile hut, and we fled to higher land. I could not let the rains destroy our next home. After much thought, I remembered the luxury Gianni houseboats that one of my father's companies had built. I would build a house that would anchor securely on the shore of the river. It would float when the rainstorms came and protect us from wild animals at night.

Although I built the houseboat with Ayira's help, I believed the Green Man had somehow placed the correct plans in my brain. After the next severe rainstorm, we were delighted and relieved to discover our houseboat was undamaged. Now, we could sleep without worrying about flooding and wild animals attacking us.

Chapter 9
What is most Important

Ayira and I were happy, and with her help, I learned to value all the trees, plants, animals, and insects of the rain forest. We understood how to survive in the forest without having to destroy it. We discovered which plants contained healing powers to help injuries, cure illnesses, and even save our lives—and later those of our children.

One day, I realized we had not fulfilled our primary responsibilities. The Green Man had told us to have many children and ensure they would live in harmony with the forests. At this time, I began to look at Ayira differently. She had become even more enchanting. Ayira told me she also had feelings for me. We pledged our love and lives to one another. Within a year, she gave birth to a boy, the first of our many children.

Ayira taught those who wanted to learn certain skills how to cook, make clothes, shape weapons for hunting, and the proper use of medicines. I showed others how to fish and hunt. Each one of them learned what they desired, and discovered what they were good at doing. We lived a very happy life, content with our work and each other.

When our children and were old enough to understand, we shared the Green Man's teachings. We taught them well. They respected their environment, took only what they needed from the forest, and avoided eating fruit from the forbidden tree. At the end of our lives, we believed we had fulfilled the task that the Green Man had assigned us.

In time, our children met the children of the others that the Green man had spared. And the world began again, this time with people who knew how to live with the forest, and were right with Nature and each other.

After we died, a great banyan tree with many trunks sprouted from our graves. The roots and branches were entwined like our lives and love had been. Ayira and I rest there together in peace.

Never again, in this new world, would there ever be a last rain forest.

How You Can Help Save the Rain Forest

Why Are Rain Forests Important?

Tropical rain forests are among the most important natural features on our planet. Rain forests only cover 2% of the Earth's surface, but are homes to over 50% of all species of plants and animals living here. Rain forest trees help the planet breathe by absorbing carbon dioxide (a Greenhouse Gas) from the atmosphere, and producing the oxygen that people and animals need to survive. If the Earth had lungs like human beings, the rain forests would be those lungs.

Rain forests also do the following for our world:

- They help balance the global climate.
- They provide homes to many endangered species of plants and animals.
- The tree's roots help protect against flood, drought, and erosion.
- They provide food, and also new sources for medicines to help the sick.
- They are home to many different tribes of native peoples.
- They are one of the most beautiful places we have, and show us how nature works.

How And Why Humans Are Destroying The Rain Forest

Human beings and our needs are the main reasons that rain forests are endangered. We endanger the rain forest because:

- Human beings are always trying to expand farm land to produce more food from growing crops and for land to allow cattle to graze.
- The wood in rain forest trees is a valuable thing used for fuel to burn fires, make paper, and for use in homes as siding, furniture and floors.
- Roads are being built through rain forest destroying the soil that contains the shallow roots of rain forest trees.

- Expanding needs for energy and minerals for industry.

Endangered Species Of The Rain forest

All of these animals shown here are endangered because humans are destroying their habitats. Without the rain forest, they have nowhere to go and nowhere to live. These species are only a small example of the great number that are in danger of disappearing forever.

Here are some examples of endangered animals of the rain forest:

Rio Santiago Poison Dart Frog: Its natural habitat is subtropical or tropical moist lowland rain forests. For the last decade it has been placed on the endangered species list. There are more than 100 species of poison dart frogs, varying in color and pattern. The skin of the frogs contains the poison. Poison dart frogs eat spiders and insects. Prey is captured using their long sticky tongues.

Toucan: These birds are found in South and Central America in the canopy (topmost) layer of the rain forest. There are around 40 different kinds of toucans. Toucans have large colorful bills. Though their bills are large, they are extremely lightweight. They eat nuts, berries, and other kinds of fruit. While they mostly eat fruit, they also eat insects, tree frogs, and the eggs of other birds.

3-Toed Sloth: This animal is found in the rain forest of Central and South America. Sloths move very slowly and spend most of their days sleeping and eating. They have been known to sleep up to 20 hours a day. Their main sources of nutrition are tree leaves, twigs and fruit. This diet does not provide much energy to the sloth, and is one of the reasons for its slow moving ways.

Baird's Tapir: Despite looking a bit like a pig, the tapir is actually more closely related to the horse and the rhinoceros. The tapir is a herbivore and spends it's time browsing for leaves, twigs, branches, buds, berries, and other fruits to eat. Tapirs have a long, flexible nose that they use to grab their food from trees and bushes. They are amazing swimmers and prefer to live close to water.

Green Iguana: This lizard is native to Central and South America and some of the Caribbean islands. They are 4 species of iguana worldwide. This lizard is an herbivore and eats only plant leaves and flowers. The biggest threat to the iguana's existence is human beings. Iguanas are sometimes called "chicken of the trees" and their meat is eaten for food.

Giant Anteater: This animal is also known as the "ant bear." There are four species of living anteaters. It is native to South and Central America, and eats mostly ants and termites. Sometimes they eat beetles and honey bees. Anteaters have no teeth, and do not really move their jaws. Its tongue is very long and sticky, and that is how it gets food: insects stick to it!

Macaw: Overall there are 17 different species of macaw, several of which are endangered. The macaw is a member of the parrot family and native to Central and South America. The birds are known for their bright-colored feathers that come in many different colors. The macaw is omnivorous and eats nuts and fruits along with insects, small mammals, frogs and lizards.

Golden Lion Tamarin: This animal is a small yellow-orange monkey. They mainly live in the coastal rain forest region of Brazil in South America. Golden lion tamarins are omnivorous, feeding on fruits, insects, and small lizards. It is estimated there are only 1,500 of them left in the wild.

How You Can Help

You can help save the rain forests by changing some of your habits and the way you look at things.

1. Use products made from sustainable materials like bamboo and recycled paper. A "susatainable material" is any one that can be regrown or easily obtained without harming the environment. You can also call it a "renewable resource." This means that the resouce will not run out and that future generations can continue to use it. Most of these sorts of materials come from plants or recycling.

2. Try to buy products from companies that make items from renewable materials. Also, see if the companies you buy from support the environment. Don't be afraid to ask them questions about where they get their materials, and how the way they operate their businesses impact the environment.

3. Eat less meat. A diet that has more fruits and vegetables demands less from the earth than raising animals to kill and eat.

4. Learn more about the rain forest. The more you know about something, the more you can inform other people. Learning and teaching will help us save the rain forest.

5. Support environmental organizations and other groups that promote protecting the rain forest that are trying to establish parks and preserves. Help preserve parks and recreational areas in your own town.

Additional Resources to Learn More About the Rain Forest

Books:

At Home in the Rain Forest written by Diane Willow, illustrated by Laura Jacques

How Monkeys Make Chocolate: Foods and Medicines from the Rainforests written and illustrated by Adrian Forsyth

The New 50 Simple Things Kids Can Do to Save the Earth by Sophie Javna and The Earth-Works Group

One Day in the Tropical Rain Forest by Jean Craighead George

Websites:

Forest News: a Blog by the Center for International Forestry Research (this site translates into several different languages):

blog.cifor.org/amazonia/#.UvdKhvl_uSr

Amazonas Sustainable Foundation: (this site translates into several different languages)

blog.cifor.org/amazon/#.Ux9N2fldWSp

Rain Forest Alliance:

www.rainforest-alliance.org

About the Author
Felipe Moreton Chohfi

Felipe Moreton Chohfi was born in São Paulo, Brazil in 1980. At age 11 he moved to Portugal together with his family due to his father's job. Felipe attended the Oporto British School where he wrote, at age 13, *The Last Rain Forest* in English.

Felipe then went to England where he studied and received his degree in Environmental Engineering at UWE (University of the West of England), Bristol.

Back in Brazil, Felipe earned his Masters in Renewable Energy at Universidade Federal de Itajubá. Currently, he is working on his doctorate in Bio-refinery Configurations at the University of Campinas, following his lifelong concern with and commitment towards the preservation of the Natural Environment.

Felipe has had many articles linked to environmental sustainability published in technical journals.

About the Artist
Angelo Bonito

Angelo Bonito is an award-winning illustrator who lives in São Paulo, Brazil. Angelo calls himself "a self-made artist" since he has learned everything about art on his own. He has been a professional illustrator for over thirty years, and started selling working for advertising agencies and publishers in Brazil and Europe when he was just fifteen years old.

Angelo has been honored with many awards for his work over the years. Here are some examples:

- 1997-2008: Gold award, highly recommended category by the Br Brazil National Book Foundation for Children and Youth, *Famous Children* and for a biography of Santos Dummont.
- 2004, Gold Medal, columnist Brazil, printed media Category, for his *Bank Boston campaign*
- 1985, Gold Medal, Illustration category, *Clube de Criação do Brasil*

Angelo is a very versatile artist working in digital imaging and 3D software, but also in traditional materials and techniques like oils, acrylic and watercolors.

CPSIA information can be obtained
at www.ICGtesting.com
Printed in the USA
LVIC05n1044010614
387884LV00006B/19

* 9 7 8 1 6 1 8 0 7 0 8 9 0 *